2013 Conference of the North American Chapter of the Association for Computational Linguistics: Human Language Technologies (NAACL HLT 2013)

Tutorials

Atlanta, Georgia, USA
9 June 2013

ISBN: 978-1-62748-841-9

Printed from e-media with permission by:

Curran Associates, Inc.
57 Morehouse Lane
Red Hook, NY 12571

Some format issues inherent in the e-media version may also appear in this print version.

Printed by Curran Associates, Inc. (2013)

For permission requests, please contact the Association for Computational Linguistics at the address below.

Association for Computational Linguistics
209 N. Eighth Street
Stroudsburg, Pennsylvania 18360

Phone: 1-570-476-8006
Fax: 1-570-476-0860

acl@aclweb.org

Additional copies of this publication are available from:

Curran Associates, Inc.
57 Morehouse Lane
Red Hook, NY 12571 USA
Phone: 845-758-0400
Fax: 845-758-2634
Email: curran@proceedings.com
Web: www.proceedings.com

Tutorial chairs

Katrin Erk, University of Texas at Austin
Jimmy Lin, University of Maryland

Table of Contents

Tutorials Program

Sunday, June 9, 2013

Morning Session

9:00–12:30 *Deep Learning for NLP (without Magic)*
Richard Socher and Christopher D. Manning

9:00–12:30 *Discourse Processing*
Manfred Stede

9:00–12:30 *NLP for uncertain data at scale*
Sameep Mehta and L V Subramaniam

Afternoon Session

2:00–5:30 *Semantic Role Labeling*
Martha Palmer, Ivan Titov and Shumin Wu

2:00–5:30 *Spectral Learning Algorithms for Natural Language Processing*
Shay Cohen, Michael Collins, Dean Foster, Karl Stratos and Lyle Ungar

2:00–5:30 *Morphological, Syntactical and Semantic Knowledge in Statistical Machine Translation*
Marta Ruiz Costa-jussà and Chris Quirk

Deep Learning for NLP (without Magic)

Richard Socher, Chris Manning
Stanford University
richard@socher.org
manning@stanford.edu

1 Overview

Machine learning is everywhere in today's NLP, but by and large machine learning amounts to numerical optimization of weights for human designed representations and features. The goal of deep learning is to explore how computers can take advantage of data to develop features and representations appropriate for complex interpretation tasks. This tutorial aims to cover the basic motivation, ideas, models and learning algorithms in deep learning for natural language processing. Recently, these methods have been shown to perform very well on various NLP tasks such as language modeling, POS tagging, named entity recognition, sentiment analysis and paraphrase detection, among others. The most attractive quality of these techniques is that they can perform well without any external hand-designed resources or time-intensive feature engineering. Despite these advantages, many researchers in NLP are not familiar with these methods. Our focus is on insight and understanding, using graphical illustrations and simple, intuitive derivations. The goal of the tutorial is to make the inner workings of these techniques transparent, intuitive and their results interpretable, rather than black boxes labeled "magic here". The first part of the tutorial presents the basics of neural networks, neural word vectors, several simple models based on local windows and the math and algorithms of training via backpropagation. In this section applications include language modeling and POS tagging. In the second section we present recursive neural networks which can learn structured tree outputs as well as vector representations for phrases and sentences. We cover both equations as well as applications. We show how training can be achieved by a modified version of the backpropagation algorithm introduced before. These modifications allow the algorithm to work on tree structures. Applications include sentiment analysis and paraphrase detection. We also draw connections to recent work in semantic compositionality in vector spaces. The principle goal, again, is to make these methods appear intuitive and interpretable rather than mathematically confusing. By this point in the tutorial, the audience members should have a clear understanding of how to build a deep learning system for word-, sentence- and document-level tasks. The last part of the tutorial gives a general overview of the different applications of deep learning in NLP, including bag of words models. We will provide a discussion of NLP-oriented issues in modeling, interpretation, representational power, and optimization.

2 Outline

Part I: The Basics

- Motivation
- From logistic regression to neural networks
- Theory: Backpropagation training
- Applications: Word vector learning, POS, NER
- Unsupervised pre-training, multi-task learning, and learning relations

PART II: Recursive Neural Networks

- Motivation
- Definition of RNNs
- Theory: Backpropagation through structure
- Applications: Sentiment Analysis, Paraphrase detection, Relation Classification

PART III: Applications and Discussion

- Overview of various NLP applications
- Efficient reconstruction or prediction of high-dimensional sparse vectors
- Discussion of future directions, advantages and limitations

3 Speaker Bios

Richard Socher[1] is a PhD student at Stanford working with Chris Manning and Andrew Ng. His research interests are machine learning for NLP and vision. He is interested in developing new models that learn useful features, capture compositional and hierarchical structure in multiple modalities and perform well across different tasks. He was awarded the 2011 Yahoo! Key Scientific Challenges Award, the Distinguished Application Paper Award at ICML 2011 and a Microsoft Research PhD Fellowship in 2012.

Christopher Manning[2] is an Associate Professor of Computer Science and Linguistics at Stanford University (PhD, Stanford, 1995). Manning has coauthored leading textbooks on statistical approaches to NLP (Manning and Schuetze 1999) and information retrieval (Manning et al. 2008). His recent work concentrates on machine learning and natural language processing, including applications such as statistical parsing and text understanding, joint probabilistic inference, clustering, and deep learning over text and images.

[1] `http://www.socher.org/`

[2] `http://nlp.stanford.edu/~manning/`

Discourse Processing

Manfred Stede
Universität Potsdam
stede@uni-potsdam.de

1 Overview

The observation that discourse is more than a mere sequence of utterances or sentences amounts to a truism. But what follows from this? In what way does the "value added" arise when segments of discourse are juxtaposed - how does hierarchical structure originate from a linearized discourse?

While many discourse phenomena apply to dialogue and monologue alike, this tutorial will center its attention on monologue written text. The perspective taken is that of practical language processing: We study methods for automatically deriving discourse information from text, and point to aspects of their implementation. The emphasis is on breadth rather than depth, so that the attendees will get an overview of the central tasks of discourse processing, with pointers to the literature for studying the individual problems in more depth. Much of the tutorial will follow the line of the recent book M. Stede: Discourse Processing. Morgan & Claypool 2011.

Specifically, we will study the most important ways of ascribing structure to discourse. This is, first, a breakdown into functional units that are characteristic for the genre of the text. A news message, for example, is conventionally structured in a different way than a scientific paper is. For grasping this level of structure, the patterns that are characteristic for the specific genre need to be modeled.

Second, an ongoing text, unless it is very short, will cover different topics and address them in a sensible linear order. This is largely independent of genre, and since the notion of topic is relatively vague, it is harder to describe and sometimes difficult to identify. The common approach is to track the distribution of content words across the text, but in addition, overt signals for topic switches can be exploited.

Third, the identification of coreference links is a central aspect of discourse processing, and has received much attention in computational linguistics. We will survey the corpus-based methods that have dominated the field in recent years, and then look at the ramifications that the set of all coreference links in a text has for its structure.

Fourth, we investigate the structure resulting from establishing coherence relations (e.g., Cause, Contrast) among adjacent text segments. The term "discourse parsing" is often used for the task of identifying such relations (by exploiting more or less explicit linguistic signals) and building tree structures that reflect the semantic or pragmatic scaffolding of a (portion of) text.

Thus emerges a picture of a text as a series of different, yet related, layers of analysis. The final part of the tutorial addresses the issue of inter-connections between these levels. As a tool for accessing such multi-layered text corpora, we will see how the (open-source) ANNIS2 database allows for querying the data across different layers, and for visualizing different structural layers in appropriate ways.

2 Outline

1. Introduction: Coherence and cohesion. How does a text differ from a "non-text"?

2. Discourse structure as induced by the genre. Not all texts are created equal: The genre can determine text structure to a large extent. We look at three examples: Court decisions, film reviews, scientific papers.

3. Topics and text structure. Few texts keep talking about just one thing: Methods for finding topic breaks.

4. Coreference and its role for text structure. For understanding a text, we need to know who and what is being referred to: Methods for coreference analysis.

5. Coherence relations and "rhetorical structure". Trees resulting from semantic or pragmatic links between text segments: Methods for discourse parsing.

6. Synopsis: Text analysis on multiple levels

7. Accessing multi-layer corpora: The ANNIS2 Database

3 Speaker Bio

Manfred Stede[1], University of Potsdam. After completing his dissertation on the role of lexical semantics in multilingual text generation, Manfred Stede shifted

[1] `http://www.ling.uni-potsdam.de/~stede/`

his research focus towards problems of discourse structure and its role in various applications of text understanding. For discourse structure, his work centered on coherence relations and associated structural descriptions of text, and on the linguistic signals of such relations, especially connectives. From the early 2000s on, he developed the Potsdam Commentary Corpus as an example of (German) texts analyzed simultaneously on multiple levels, including sentential syntax, coreference, and rhetorical structure; in parallel, the technical infrastructure of a database for querying and visualizing multi-layer corpora was developed. In recent years, more analysis levels have been added to the corpus (e.g., content zones, connectives and their arguments). As for applications, Manfred worked on text summarization and various tasks of information extraction; more recently, his focus has been on issues of subjectivity and sentiment analysis.

Towards Reliability-Aware Entity Analytics and Integration for Noisy Text at Scale

Sameep Mehta, L. Venkata Subramaniam
IBM Research India
sameepmehta, lvsubram@in.ibm.com

1 Outline

Due to easy to use apps (Facebook, Twitter, etc.), higher Internet connectivity and always on facility allowed by smart phones, the key characteristics of raw data are changing. This new data can be characterized by 4V's - Volume, Velocity, Variety and Veracity. For example during a Football match, some people will Tweet about goals, penalties, etc., while others may write longer blogs and further there will be match reports filed in trusted online news media after the match. Although the sources may be varied, the data describes and provides multiple evidences for the same event. Such multiple evidences should be used to strengthen the belief in the underlying physical event as the individual data points may have inherent uncertainty. The uncertainty can arise from inconsistent, incomplete and ambiguous reports. The uncertainty is also because the trust levels of the different sources vary and affect the overall reliability. We will summarize various efforts to perform reliability aware entity integration.

The other problem in text analysis in such setting is posed by presence of noise in the text. Since the text is produced in several informal settings such as email, blogs, tweet, SMS, chat and is inherently noisy and has several veracity issues. For example, missing punctuation and the use of non-standard words can often hinder standard natural language processing techniques such as part-of-speech tagging and parsing. Further downstream applications such as entity extraction, entity resolution and entity completion have to explicitly handle noise in order to return useful results. Often, depending on the application, noise can be modeled and it may be possible to develop specific strategies to immunize the system from the effects of noise and improve performance. Also the aspect of reliability is key as a lot of this data is ambiguous, incomplete, conflicting, untrustworthy and deceptive.

The key goals of this tutorial are:

1. Draw the attention of researchers towards methods for doing entity analytics and integration on data with 4V characteristics.
2. Differentiate between noise and uncertainty in such data.
3. Provide an in-depth discussion on handling noise in NLP based methods.
4. Finally, handling uncertainty through information fusion and integration.

This tutorial builds on two earlier tutorials: NAACL 2010 tutorial on Noisy Text and COMAD 2012 tutorial on Reliability Aware Data Fusion. In parallel the authors are also hosting a workshop on related topic "Reliability Aware Data Fusion" at SIAM Data Mining Conference, 2013.

2 Outline

2.1 Data with 4V characteristics

- Define Volume, Velocity, Variety and Veracity and metrics to quantify them
- Information extraction on data with 4V characteristics

2.2 Key technical challenges posed by the 4V dimensions and linguistics techniques to address them

- Analyzing streaming text
- Large scale distributed algorithms for NLP
- Integrating structured and unstructured data
- Noisy text analytics
- Reliability
- Use case: Generating single view of entity from social data

2.3 Computing Reliability and Trust

- Computing source reliability
- Identifying Trust Worthy Messages
- Data fusion to improve reliability: Probabilistic data fusion, information measures, evidential reasoning
- Use case: Event detection using social data, news and online sources

3 Speaker Bios

Sameep Mehta[1] is researcher in Information Management Group at IBM Research India. He received his M.S. and Ph.D. from The Ohio State University, USA in 2006. He also holds an Adjunct Faculty position at the International Institute of Information Technology, New Delhi. Sameep regularly advises MS and PhD students at University of Delhi and IIT Delhi. He regularly delivers Tutorials at COMAD (2009, 2010 and 2011). His current research interests include Data Mining, Business Analytics, Service Science, Text Mining, and Workforce Optimization.

L. Venkata Subramaniam[2] manages the information management analytics and solutions group at IBM Research India. He received his PhD from IIT Delhi in 1999. His research focuses on unstructured information management, statistical natural language processing, noisy text analytics, text and data mining, information theory, speech and image processing. He often teaches and guides student thesis at IIT Delhi on these topics. His tutorial titled Noisy Text Analytics was the second largest at NAACL-HLT 2010. He co founded the AND (Analytics for Noisy Unstructured Text Data) workshop series and also co-chaired the first four workshops, 2007-2010. He was guest co-editor of two special issues on Noisy Text Analytics in the International Journal of Document Analysis and Recognition in 2007 and 2009.

[1] http://in.linkedin.com/in/sameepmehta
[2] https://sites.google.com/site/lvs004/

Semantic Role Labeling

Martha Palmer*, Ivan Titov§, Shumin Wu*
*University of Colorado
§Saarland University
Martha.Palmer@colorado.edu
titovian,wushumin@gmail.com

1 Overview

This tutorial will describe semantic role labeling, the assignment of semantic roles to eventuality participants in an attempt to approximate a semantic representation of an utterance. The linguistic background and motivation for the definition of semantic roles will be presented, as well as the basic approach to semantic role annotation of large amounts of corpora. Recent extensions to this approach that encompass light verb constructions and predicative adjectives will be included, with reference to their impact on English, Arabic, Hindi and Chinese. Current proposed extensions such as Abstract Meaning Representations and richer event representations will also be touched on.

Details of machine learning approaches will be provided, beginning with fully supervised approaches that use the annotated corpora as training material. The importance of syntactic parse information and the contributions of different feature choices, including tree kernels, will be discussed, as well as the advantages and disadvantages of particular machine learning algorithms and approaches such as joint inference. Appropriate considerations for evaluation will be presented as well as successful uses of semantic role labeling in NLP applications.

We will also cover techniques for exploiting unlabeled corpora and transferring models across languages. These include methods, which project annotations across languages using parallel data, induce representations solely from unlabeled corpora (unsupervised methods) or exploit a combination of a small amount of human annotation and a large unlabeled corpus (semi-supervised techniques). We will discuss methods based on different machine learning paradigms, including generative Bayesian models, graph-based algorithms and bootstrapping style techniques.

2 Outline

I. Introduction, background and annotation

- Motivation – who did what to whom
- Linguistic Background
- Basic Annotation approach
- Recent extensions
- Language Specific issues with English, Arabic, Hindi and Chinese
- Semlink – Mapping between PropBank, VerbNet and FrameNet.
- The next step – Events and Abstract Meaning Representations

II. Supervised Machine Learning for SRL

- Identification and Classification
- Features (tree kernel, English vs. Chinese)
- Choice of ML method and feature combinations (kernel vs feature space)
- Joint Inference
- Impact of Parsing
- Evaluation
- Applications (including multi-lingual)

III. Semi-supervised and Unsupervised Approaches

- Cross-lingual annotation projection methods and direct transfer of SRL models across languages
- Semi-supervised learning methods
- Unsupervised induction
- Adding supervision and linguistic priors to unsupervised methods

3 Speaker Bios

Martha Palmer[1] is a Professor of Linguistics and Computer Science, and a Fellow of the Institute of Cognitive Science at the University of Colorado. Her current research is aimed at building domain-independent and language independent techniques for semantic interpretation based on linguistically annotated data, such as Proposition Banks. She has been the PI on NSF, NIH and DARPA projects for linguistic annotation (syntax, semantics and pragmatics) of English, Chinese, Korean, Arabic and Hindi. She has been a member of the Advisory Committee for the DARPA TIDES program, Chair of SIGLEX, Chair of SIGHAN, a past President of the Association for Computational Linguistics, and is a Co-Editor of JNLE and of LiLT and is on the CL Editorial Board. She received her Ph.D. in Artificial Intelligence from the University of Edinburgh in 1985.

Ivan Titov[2] joined the Saarland University as a junior faculty and head of a research group in November 2009, following a postdoc at the University of Illinois at Urbana-Champaign. He received his Ph.D. in Computer Science from the University of Geneva in 2008 and his master's degree in Applied Mathematics and Informatics from the St. Petersburg State Polytechnic University (Russia) in 2003. His research interests are in statistical natural language processing (models of syntax, semantics and sentiment) and machine learning (structured prediction methods, latent variable models, Bayesian methods).

Shumin Wu is a Computer Science PhD student (advised by Dr. Martha Palmer) at the University of Colorado. His current research is aimed at developing and applying semantic mapping (aligning and jointly inferring predicate-argument structures between languages) to Chinese dropped-pronoun recovery/alignment, automatic verb class induction, and other applications relevant to machine translation.

[1] `http://verbs.colorado.edu/~mpalmer/`

[2] `http://people.mmci.uni-saarland.de/~titov/`

Spectral Learning Algorithms for Natural Language Processing

Shay Cohen*, Michael Collins*, Dean P. Foster§, Karl Stratos*, Lyle Ungar§
*Columbia University
§University of Pennsylvania
scohen,mcollins,stratos@cs.columbia.edu
dean@foster.net
ungar@cis.upenn.edu

1 Introduction

Recent work in machine learning and NLP has developed spectral algorithms for many learning tasks involving latent variables. Spectral algorithms rely on singular value decomposition as a basic operation, usually followed by some simple estimation method based on the method of moments. From a theoretical point of view, these methods are appealing in that they offer consistent estimators (and PAC-style guarantees of sample complexity) for several important latent-variable models. This is in contrast to the EM algorithm, which is an extremely successful approach, but which only has guarantees of reaching a local maximum of the likelihood function.

From a practical point of view, the methods (unlike EM) have no need for careful initialization, and have recently been shown to be highly efficient (as one example, in work under submission by the authors on learning of latent-variable PCFGs, a spectral algorithm performs at identical accuracy to EM, but is around 20 times faster).

2 Outline

In this tutorial we will aim to give a broad overview of spectral methods, describing theoretical guarantees, as well as practical issues. We will start by covering the basics of singular value decomposition and describe efficient methods for doing singular value decomposition. The SVD operation is at the core of most spectral algorithms that have been developed.

We will then continue to cover canonical correlation analysis (CCA). CCA is an early method from statistics for dimensionality reduction. With CCA, two or more views of the data are created, and they are all projected into a lower dimensional space which maximizes the correlation between the views. We will review the basic algorithms underlying CCA, give some formal results giving guarantees for latent-variable models and also describe how they have been applied recently to learning lexical representations from large quantities of unlabeled data. This idea of learning lexical representations can be extended further, where unlabeled data is used to learn underlying representations which are subsequently used as additional information for supervised training.

We will also cover how spectral algorithms can be used for structured prediction problems with sequences and parse trees. A striking recent result by Hsu, Kakade and Zhang (2009) shows that HMMs can be learned efficiently using a spectral algorithm. HMMs are widely used in NLP and speech, and previous algorithms (typically based on EM) were guaranteed to only reach a local maximum of the likelihood function, so this is a crucial result. We will review the basic mechanics of the HMM learning algorithm, describe its formal guarantees, and also cover practical issues.

Last, we will cover work about spectral algorithms in the context of natural language parsing. We will show how spectral algorithms can be used to estimate the parameter models of latent-variable PCFGs, a model which serves as the base for state-of-the-art parsing models such as the one of Petrov et al. (2007). We will show what are the practical steps that are needed to be taken in order to make spectral algorithms for L-PCFGs (or other models in general) practical and comparable to state of the art.

3 Speaker Bios

Shay Cohen[1] is a postdoctoral research scientist in the Department of Computer Science at Columbia University. He is a computing innovation fellow. His research interests span a range of topics in natural language processing and machine learning. He is especially interested in developing efficient and scalable parsing algorithms as well as learning algorithms for probabilistic grammars.

Michael Collins[2] is the Vikram S. Pandit Professor of computer science at Columbia University. His research is focused on topics including statistical parsing, structured prediction problems in machine learning, and applications including machine translation, dialog systems, and speech recognition. His awards include a

[1] http://www.cs.columbia.edu/~scohen/

[2] http://www.cs.columbia.edu/~mcollins/

Sloan fellowship, an NSF career award, and best paper awards at EMNLP (2002, 2004, and 2010), UAI (2004 and 2005), and CoNLL 2008.

Dean P. Foster[3] is currently the Marie and Joseph Melone Professor of Statistics at the Wharton School of the University of Pennsylvania. His current research interests are machine learning, stepwise regression and computational linguistics. He has been searching for new methods of finding useful features in big data sets. His current set of hammers revolve around fast matrix methods (which decompose 2nd moments) and tensor methods for decomposing 3rd moments.

Karl Stratos[4] is a Ph.D. student in the Department of Computer Science at Columbia. His research is focused on machine learning and natural language processing. His current research efforts are focused on spectral learning of latent-variable models, or more generally, uncovering latent structure from data.

Lyle Ungar[5] is a professor at the Computer and Information Science Department at the University of Pennsylvania. His research group develops scalable machine learning and text mining methods, including clustering, feature selection, and semi-supervised and multi-task learning for natural language, psychology, and medical research. Example projects include spectral learning of language models, multi-view learning for gene expression and MRI data, and mining social media to better understand personality and well-being.

[3]http://gosset.wharton.upenn.edu/~foster/index.pl

[4]http://www.cs.columbia.edu/~stratos/

[5]http://www.cis.upenn.edu/~ungar/

Morphological, Syntactical and Semantic Knowledge in Statistical Machine Translation

Marta R. Costa-jussà*, Chris Quirk§
*Institute for Infocomm Research
§Microsoft Research
martaruizcostajussa@gmail.com
chrisq@microsoft.com

1 Overview

This tutorial focuses on how morphology, syntax and semantics may be introduced into a standard phrase-based statistical machine translation system with techniques such as machine learning, parsing and word sense disambiguation, among others.

Regarding the phrase-based system, we will describe only the key theory behind it. The main challenges of this approach are that the output contains unknown words, wrong word orders and non-adequate translated words. To solve these challenges, recent research enhances the standard system using morphology, syntax and semantics.

Morphologically-rich languages have many different surface forms, even though the stem of a word may be the same. This leads to rapid vocabulary growth, as various prefixes and suffixes can combine with stems in a large number of possible combinations. Language model probability estimation is less robust because many more word forms occur rarely in the data. This morphologically-induced sparsity can be reduced by incorporating morphological information into the SMT system. We will describe the three most common solutions to face morphology: preprocessing the data so that the input language more closely resembles the output language; using additional language models that introduce morphological information; and post-processing the output to add proper inflections.

Syntax differences between the source and target language may lead to significant differences in the relative word order of translated words. Standard phrase-based SMT systems surmount reordering/syntactic challenges by learning from data. Most approaches model reordering inside translation units and using statistical methodologies, which limits the performance in language pairs with different grammatical structures. We will briefly introduce some recent advances in

SMT that use modeling approaches based on principles more powerful flat phrases and better suited to the hierarchical structures of language: SMT decoding with stochastic synchronous context free grammars and syntax-driven translation models.

Finally, semantics are not directly included in the SMT core algorithm, which means that challenges such as polysemy or synonymy are either learned directly from data or they are incorrectly translated. We will focus on recent attempts to introduce semantics into statistical-based systems by using source context information.

The course material will be suitable both for attendees with limited knowledge of the field, and for researchers already familiar with SMT who wish to learn about modern tendencies in hybrid SMT. The mathematical content of the course include probability and simple machine learning, so reasonable knowledge of statistics and mathematics is required. There will be a small amount of linguistics and ideas from natural language processing.

2 Outline

1. Statistical Machine Translation
   - Introduction to Machine Translation approaches
   - Phrase-based systems
2. Morphology in SMT
   - Types of languages in terms of morphology
   - Enriching source language
   - Inflection generation
   - Class-based language models
3. Syntax in SMT
4. Semantics in SMT
   - Sense disambiguation
   - Context-dependent translations

3 Speaker Bios

Marta R. Costa-jussà[1], Institute for Infocomm Research (I2R), is a Telecommunication's Engineer by the Universitat Politècnica de Catalunya (UPC, Barcelona) and she received her PhD from the UPC in 2008. Her research experience is mainly in Automatic Speech Recognition, Machine Translation and Information Retrieval. She has worked at LIMSI-CNRS (Paris), Barcelona Media Innovation Center (Barcelona) and the Universidade de Sao Paulo (São Paulo). Since December 2012 she is working at Institute for Infocomm Research (Singapore) implementing the IMTraP project ("Integration of Machine Translation Paradigms") on Hybrid Machine Translation, funded by the European Marie Curie International Outgoing European Fellowship program. She is currently organizing the ACL Workshop HyTRA 2013 and she will be teaching a summer school course on hybrid machine translation at ESSLLI 2013.

Chris Quirk[2], Microsoft Research. After studying Computer Science and Mathematics at Carnegie Mellon University, Chris joined Microsoft in 2000 to work on the Intentional Programming project, an extensible compiler and development framework. He moved to the Natural Language Processing group in 2001, where his research has mostly focused on statistical machine translation powering Microsoft Translator, especially on several generations of a syntax directed translation system that powers over half of the translation systems. He is also interested in semantic parsing, paraphrase methods, and very practical problems such as spelling correction and transliteration.

[1] `http://www.costa-jussa.com`

[2] `http://research.microsoft.com/en-us/people/chrisq/`

Author Index